To My [   ]

on our FIRST CHRISTMAS,

THIS BOOK IS FOR YOU

AND YOUR PRECIOUS CHILDREN

WHOM I HAVE GROWN TO

LOVE AND CHERISH. I HONOR

YOUR INNOCENCE AND THE

GIFT OF ALL OF YOU IN MY

LIFE. Love,

YOUR HUSBAND,

Rich

God's Precious Girl
A Celebration of Spirituality

By Mary Lowe Williams

Photography by Connie Palen

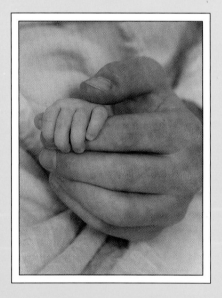

Health Communications, Inc.
Deerfield Beach, Florida

Warmth and Wonder for God's Precious Girl . . .

We invite you to share the warmth and wonder of Mary Lowe Williams' tender affirmations and Connie Palen's beautiful photographs which illuminate the uniqueness of every girl.

This lovely book powerfully, yet gently, affirms that all children are valuable, and deserve love and acceptance.

God's Precious Girl is a gift of love for children from 4 to 104. It touches the heart and soothes the spirit. Frequently read this book to your child or yourself and honor the preciousness in each of us.

We are delighted to share these spiritual affirmations with you, and hope they bring you many moments of serenity.

Health Communications, Inc.

©1992 Mary Lowe Williams
ISBN 1-55874-247-6

Publisher: Health Communications, Inc.
          3201 S.W. 15th Street
          Deerfield Beach, Florida 33442-8190

Dedicated to my daughter, Marla . . . .
May the laughter of a child bring
you the joy of God.

Am I really a precious child of God?

My mother says that God
loves me, and that God
will *always* love me.

And God blesses me every day:

Thank you, God, for my Koala Bear.
Thank you for my house.
Thank you for my clothes.
Thank you for my dolls.
Thank you for my toys.
Thank you for Mom and Dad.
Thank you for my brother.
Thank you for me.
I love you, God.
Sometimes I wish I could see you, God.
Thank you for everything.
I am so happy.

Marla D. Williams, age 3

Thank you for loving me God.

God is a mystery to me:

Who made God?
Does God have a face?
Is God black or white, brown or yellow?
Does God get hungry?
What language does God speak?
Can God make my friend well again?
Is God a man or woman?

My father thinks God may
always be a mystery.
I *like* mysteries.

I am amazed at God's wonderful creation.

I want to enjoy God,
wherever God
is found.

*I can feel God
in my heart.*

I love knowing God
is always near.

*I love to giggle and
have fun.*

Part of God's plan is for
me to be happy.

All my feelings are important to God.

No matter how I feel, God accepts me just the way I am.

*There are times when I am
afraid to do things
by myself.*

Yet I feel safe because
God looks after me.

*Sometimes everyone is
too busy for me.*

God puts many wonderful people
in my life. When someone
listens to me, I feel
important.

I try to do *things to please my parents and friends but sometimes they are still unhappy.*

My gift to others is *to be* myself, just as I am, the wonderful person God created. Even though I try, I may not be able to make someone else happy.

Sometimes I am angry and don't get along with others.

God wants me to say how I feel. Because I want others to listen to me, I will listen to them. We can ask each other for what we want, and learn to give and take.

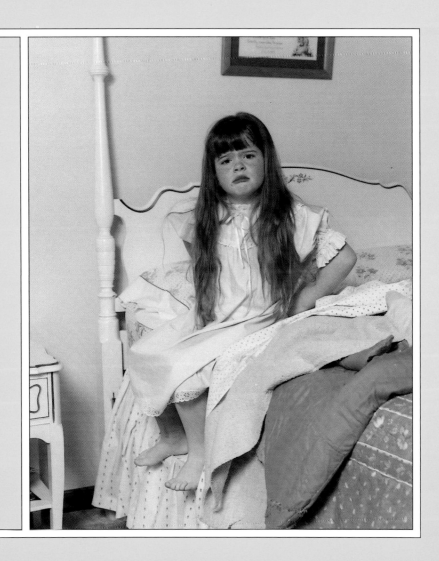

I wish I didn't make mistakes.

Making mistakes does not mean I am bad.
God knows making mistakes is the way
to learn. It means I need more time
and practice at something. I will
love myself, mistakes and all,
just as God loves me.

I especially feel bad when
my mistakes hurt
someone else.

Yet being angry with myself only
makes me feel worse. When
I say, "I'm sorry," and give
the person time to get
over being hurt, we
both feel better.

*I wish I could do what
my friend does.*

God gives each of us different
abilities. I need to remember
that I can do some things
my friend cannot.

*I am glad that God
made me a girl.*

God also gives me the abilities
and freedom to become
whatever I desire.

*When I am proud of
something I do, I
feel joyful and
excited.*

God's spirit inside me says,
"You did it! Good job!"

My laughing, singing and dancing show God my thanks.

When I show how thankful
I am, God is pleased.

I like to talk to God.

We are good friends.

*I can ask God for what
I need and want.*

I am learning to trust that God
knows best, and will give me
what I need when the
time is right.

God wants me to
love myself.

Loving myself feels good and
makes it easier to love
and accept others.

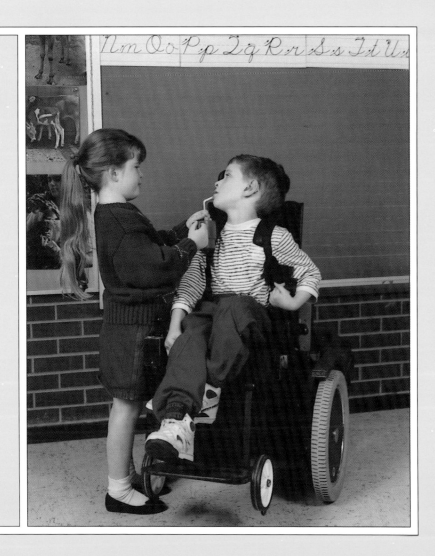

*I feel calm and
peaceful.*

Thank you, God, for your
presence in my life.

Yes, I am a precious child of God.

Always.

More Valuable Resources From Mary L. Williams

I AM PRECIOUS relaxation and affirmation audiotapes for adults and children.

Slides of *MY PRECIOUS CHILD, GOD'S PRECIOUS BOY* and *GOD'S PRECIOUS GIRL* for professional use.

Lectures and workshops on dysfunctional families and on spirituality.

Write to:
  Mary L. Williams
  LOVING MATTERS
  Box 1524
  Glenwood Springs, CO 81602